Thoughts Of A Man

Paul-Arthur Mays

BookLeaf Publishing

Presentation by *BookLeaf Publishing*

Web: www.bookleafpub.com

E-mail: info@bookleafpub.com

ISBN: 9789357744959

First edition 2023

For My Dad. I Love You.

PREFACE

Allow Yourself To Delve Into The Uncommon.
You May Find What You're Looking For.

Watashi no saiaku no akumu

The chains hold him bound
Gripping, Clutches onto his soul
Rains pour from inside
Invisible he
Waiting, hoping for better
Darkness all around
Glacier blade in deep
Swiftly poison river run
Antibody faints
Chaos erupts in
Magma swallows pure life force
Energy has died
Two snakes circle the rod
Celestial sent
Death by broken heart
Thousand Eyes confused
Fretful they tremble away
Time to heal alone.

4

Hello, Little One.
I Want To See Who You Will Be.
Please, Show Me.
Almost Done, Big One.

Come, Little One.
Time For Your Meal.
Happy, Joyful The Squeal.
Yes, Big One.

Eat, Little One.
Plate, Spork, And Juice
Don't Let The Napkin Loose.
Thank You, Big One.

Go Little One.
Learn The Day.
Soar And Grow Away.
I'll See You, Big One.

Hey, Little One,
It's Time To Go.
Don't Be Sad, I Know.
I'm Ok. I Love You, Big One.

Oh, Little One
My Heart Smiles Wide.
My Faith In You Will Abide.
Thank You, Little One.

Silent Knight

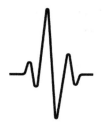

Strong, Silent Is He.
Knows Not A Soul
Anguish The Toll
Is It Me?

Why Are You?
Eyes Blue, Red Head.
Step Alive, Yet Pace Dead.
The Battle Sad, Yet True.

I Speak Not
Words Are Your Maze
Stunned Gaze
Yelling Is My Thought.

Angry Are You?
Why Should I Tell?
Black Ears Will My Words Fell
Away From Me Should You.

Cloak

Show You Love Will I?
Heart Manipulating
Silent Will I Be.

Dagger

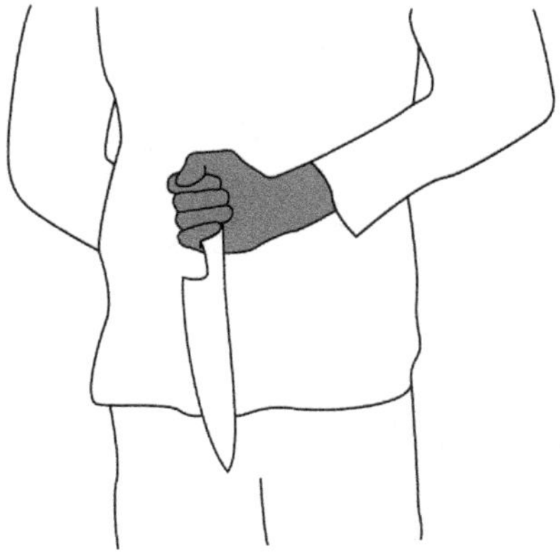

Darkness Mighty Strike
Unconscious The Quite Blue Soul
Surprised At Black Depth

Lady Of The Lake

Step Into My World.
Waves Long and Curled.
Don't Be Afraid.
Come, Let Us Wade.

Look Upon The Lake With Me.
Soft The Breeze Flows Calmly
Take My Hand
I'll Show You Away From Your Barren Land.

Will You Dance?
Said With The Soft Glance.
Her Hand Sweeps My Cheek.
Heart Flutters Me Happily Weak.

How Should I Move?
To What Groove?
Just Flow With The Wave
Steady Your Pace, Lower Your Stave.

Graceful We Shall Walk In The Clear.
Come Along My Dear.
A Waltz On The Water
We Shall Not Falter.

Invisible We To They
We Shall Be Lost All Day.
This Is My Will, No Mistake.
For I Am The Lady Of The Lake.

Scorch

Twelve, Conception Soul
Incinerate New Type Me
Master I Am Now.

Scour

Terror Is The Rain
Ostentatious, Maybe So
Respect Elevate.

Heart

Captivation, Oh
Flutters Floater Up Under
Seldom Undersight

Alter-Ego

Twelve Is Now Demise
Servant Of Chaos And Heart
Decimate His Life.

Purple Wave

Grip, Stand, Stunned.
Thoughts Scattered
Mind Battered
No Words For They Will Be Shunned.

Must Break The You
Must Settle Down Now
Yet, Musn't Bow
Can I Break Through?

Demise Dagger Drawn
Enemy Steadies On The Board
Soldiers Attack As The Hoard
Other Side Must Go The Pawn

Smirk And Grin He Does
Chops And Excitement Delight
Gettysburg Fight
Tighten The Gloves.

Orange

Ghosts Deployed To Me
Obliterate The Mental
Hollow Became I.

First Light

Breath Of The Ocean
Slowly Comes The Beginning
Lighthouse Rings The Bell.

3

Double Time D
Fulfill Double Dream Galore
Crowns Around Ascend

Bulldog

One Begins The Chase
Looking For Embrace
Seeks The Gail
Yet, He Flail.

Two Is Base
Articulate The Case
Speaker Of The Truth
Acceptance Of It? No. Poof.

Three Is Anticipation.
Lay The Foundation.
Growth Is Now Imminent
Old Lessons Still Permanent

Four Is Here!! Cheers Galore.
Are You Ready To See What's In Store?
Though I Missed The Big Dance,
I Must Go Forward On Life's Straight Glance.

Next In The Que

Game Time, Let's Go!!
Crowd Walks
Emcee Talks
Stop, Will We Know?

Pause The Sound.
Stops The Crowd.
3 Spoken Aloud.
Scattered They Go Around.

There's A Two, A Pair.
Stop And See
I Shall Go And Be Three
Yet, Comes An Unknown Glare.

Zooming Comes She
Sight Was Unaware
Little Did I Know There
What Would Come To Be.

Struggle, Then Concede.
Victory Is Theirs.
Ominous Are The Glares
Answers I Need.

He Now Talks, "The Culprit Is You!"
Anger Swells In The End
I Can't Comprehend!!
Now His Face Is Next In The Que.

“Peace.” Says The Inner One.
Silence Seals My Lips
Hear The Wise Tips.
Just Walk Away. Be Done.

Swiss

Oh The Great And Wise
Queen Of Generations You
Essence Is Thy Feel.

Dream

Laying On The Moon
Universe Unlimited
Limitless Lifeline

Printed in the USA
CPSIA information can be obtained
at www.ICGtesting.com
LVHW020402130524
779982LV00011B/522

9 789357 744959